The Rules of Being Highly Productive

Deepak Gupta

Published by Inspirational Publishing, 2021.

Table of Contents

THE

RULES
OF BEING
HIGHLY
PRODUCTIVE

DEEPAK GUPTA

Copyright © Deepak Gupta 2021

All rights reserved.
© Cover Design

Deepak Gupta asserts the moral right to be identified as the author of this book.

This book is partially a work of fiction. The names, characters, and incidents portrayed in it are the product of the author's imagination. Any resemblance to an actual person, living or dead, or events or localities is entirely coincidental.

Also by Deepak Gupta

30 Minutes Read Series

The Habit of Positivity 2021
The Therapy of Peace 2020
The Anti-Suicidal Self Help Book 2020
Ideas & Origami 2020
Sell Your Talent 2020
Hard Decisions Easy Life 2020
One Second Rule 2020
How to Deal with Haters 2020
Being Busy is not always Productive 2020
Happiness without Cause 2020
Alone Than Lonely 2020
How to Heal Yourself 2020

10 Principles Series

10 Principles to Beat Failure 2018
10 Principles to Love Yourself 2019
10 Principles to Live Peacefully 2021 (Upcoming Release)

Self Help Special Editions

Beta 2020 2020
5 Principles to Dig Out Success 2019
Powerful Quotes 2019
Average Mind 2019

The Power Series

The Power of Universe 2019
The Power of Nothing 2018

Classic Fiction Short Stories

The Girl with No Dreams 2019
The Pigeon with Broken Legs 2020
Two Friends in a Boat 2020

Crime Mystery & Thriller

The Man who Forgets 2019
When Queen Drowns 2019
Revenge 2019
The Lost Child 2018
Zero Degree 2018

Poetry & Prose

She's the Sunflower 2019
Wild Wife 2018
Broken with Love 2018

Science Fiction

Skyfall 2018
Earth 2200 2018

Romance & Thriller

Crushed Under Her Crush: Book 1 2020
I Can't Unlove You: Book 2 2020
Revolutionary Love 2016

Women Contemporary

She 2017

Debut Book

Inspiring Life 2015

Prologue

A virtuous man doesn't need to tell about his productivity. It reflects in his schedule.

The prologue is the most hated part for any writer because he feels confused when someone forces him to write the gist of the unabridged book in a few paragraphs. Writers communicate prologue at the start but I write it at the end to get readers aware of what they will read ahead. *This book is simple in writing yet complicated in many ways.* It's simple for those who really trust my ideas and complicated for those who think of this book as day dreaming. *That's so rude of me. I'm not rude, I'm straight forward and that's the first rule of being highly productive.* A man who wants to schedule his time, need to be rude about it. As when I was writing, this book swapped my life a lot. It stretched my mind and helped me to understand prominent lessons. *Success is not the secret but the disciplined work of a warrior who accepts everything in the phase of life.* You see contrasting life than mine but I will try to show your life from the perspective of my life. I keep it simple so everyone can recognize the track while moving on it. *Grab your notepad and a pencil because the foremost step of being highly productive is to listen to people when they talk. Most people don't read & listen.*

If you read my books easily then it doesn't mean it's easy to write. I present my ideas in a simple way. I aim to communicate with everyone. I don't want to give this book a sense of time pass but a moment to understand the flow of time. Sometimes the unadorned sentences need to read again & again to understand & absorb the real idea of people.

People don't do what they actually do. Read it again.
Much Gratitude & Love
Deepak Gupta

Chapter 1

Four Dots of being Highly Productive

The best way to reduce bad habits is to start adopting good habits.

Do you ever feel astonished that how most popular celebrities including Jeff Bezos, J.K. Rowling, Mark Zuckerberg, Warren Buffet, Elon Musk, and many more do the highly rugged work efficiently and in a very peaceful manner? When we were playing with toys, Mark Zuckerberg created Facebook and became a billionaire in no time. We don't give attention to the productive personalities but believe when we experience their results in a very less time. We believe the results and start to follow them. **Real-time management is about mounting the high priority for substantial goals. Getting successful in small goals can be a part of your success but becoming highly successful and to enter the productivity club, we have to maintain our productivity for a long time.** People cherish us for results, consistency, and dedication.

I read a lot books to increase productivity but a rare one tells the real truth about being extremely productive. People talk about the actions that work and bring results to them. There should be something ordinary in extraordinary which a normal person can also follow and determine his path. **Without taking much of your time, we are demonstrating the four dots rule of being highly productive in life.**

Four Dots - Procrastination - Origin - Productive – Highly Productive

People procrastinate when their procrastination becomes significant than their goals. When a person ceases of being highly productive, he shouldn't return to the stage of procrastination but stay at the point of origin because procrastination is a kind of continuous comfort zone of humans and **it lures us like a naked girl**. Don't try to jump from the point of procrastination to highly productive mode. There is no such stage like the last day you were productive and the next day you become a man of value. **First, set your indestructible goals that can become the tough reason to leave the bed of procrastination.** People don't compete when they don't have the value of competition. Setting big goals helps us to convert our motivation into practice and reality. Every consistent right work has results and what we all believe in. First, stop delay in your work and reach the level of origin. It's the breakeven point where you aren't wasting the time. ***When you stop squandering your time, you will surely scrounge the goals and try to work on them. Stay there. Do it consistently.*** We are saying to stay there and do it every day and don't lose the charm in any way. Celebrate it. Now, it's time for being highly productive. When a person is productive, he can make the way of finding new more productive ways and start to enjoy it more. If a plump man wants to have six-pack abs, he would need to get to restore the natural state of being slim first by walking and running every day. There's no logic to jump the steps because it may take us far away from our goals and start to accumulate stress. *When you jump all the four dots, your thoughts will surely improve. Moreover, don't forget to set the goals that can make you strong every day.*

If you need the inspiration to work, don't do it. - Elon Musk.

Chapter 2

Fool Your Mind - 125% Rule

You know, being highly productive is like to utilize our genuine potential. **Most people don't know their actual potential because they never utilized it like hell in their work.** Humans can work round the clock until they are exhausted. Elon Musk utilizes his right potential of over 100 hours a week. It's laughable because jobholders usually utilize 50 hours a week. Why there's a need to work more even when there's no pressure for work. Okay, come to the point. **A man work more under less pressure but work less under more pressure.** Less stressed people can work for more time. We call them productive people who utilize their full potential without getting affected and doubting their work. If we waste four hours a day, it means we are losing double hours of productivity. *The first four hours to waste in it and the other four hours to overcome with it.* That's why we said, be productive to reach the level of being highly productive. Utilize your real potential. Utilizing 80-90 hours a week to your right goals is pretty achievable.

When we think we are geniuses we lose half of the information and also lose the chance of being a prominent genius. Always try to do 125% of your everyday goals. We know it's more than our will but there are certain reasons. In the current scenario, people don't appreciate us every day but there's the chance to lead ourselves. And there's nothing better than to do a little more work to pat your back. Our mind is not always well pleased with the accomplishment of 100% of our daily goals but with something extra beyond it. It's kind to fool our mind to do more productive work. When we would get ready for the next day's work, we had already completed 25% of the last day and our mind would get satisfied. Don't leave the work, just because you have done a lot. **Get back to your work and do more for the next day and this will continue to motivate you consistently.**

Walk out of a meeting or drop off calls as soon as it is obvious you aren't adding value. It is not rude to leave, it's rude to make someone stay and waste their time. - Elon Musk.

Chapter 3

The Extraordinary People with Ordinary Rules

Many people think, to become extraordinary like Albert Einstein, Jack Ma, Socrates, and many brilliant philosophers need extraordinary work but the fact is wrong somewhere. **Extraordinary people have the habits of ordinary people but on a strict basis.** Extraordinary people do a lot of ordinary work but with consistency and discipline. It's easy to adopt a strict schedule for a day but difficult to maintain for a long time. We call them extraordinary because they reflect the real productivity for lifetime. Reading for a day is an ordinary habit. Reading for the whole life is an extraordinary habit. Warren Buffet reads around 500 pages a day including the stock market, company's financial statements, books, and many reputed newspapers. When he reads, he doesn't entertain meetings. J.K Rowling has a strict schedule to write from 9 AM to 3 PM. Everyone should strict about their work schedule. Dwayne Johnson who is also known as Rock wanders throughout the world but never forgets to execute his daily workout. He undertakes workout every morning and sometimes in the evening when he misses it for some reason. Rock's team Iron Paradise has established gym at every place and it doesn't matter where he goes, he gets his 45000 pounds of gym equipments ready at every place.

Don't be indolent about your tasks and do your foremost to follow the goals strictly. You are extraordinary when you follow the consistency of ordinary rules.

Chapter 4

How to enjoy Money & Life consistently

Give millions to a lazy man, and he would destroy it. Give thousands to a productive man, he would make millions.

Suppose you hit the jackpot of 1 million and now you don't have to work for a lifetime. You just have to enjoy money and have the great opportunity to roam all over the world. Looking demented and fascinating, but let me tell you, just like a man is worn-out while working, he can also get exhausted while enjoying something for free. Humans are peculiar that's why we need to think and dynamic with our rules. **A lazy man can't enjoy his money but a productive man can enjoy his necessities.**

Jeff Bezos, the world's richest man until Elon Musk have become in January 2021, keeps a schedule of his time and tasks. Why he even needs to work, he can enjoy his money, and still, it will never end. **Remember, rich people, aren't rich just because they have money. They are rich because they are productive in their work.** Jeff Bezos is a calm man and he doesn't like meetings before 10 AM. Between 10 AM to 5 PM, he takes a bulk of decisions but he takes high IQ meetings before lunch and he thinks, 'this is a great way to avoid fatigue'. A man can enjoy money when he's being productive in his work. Getting Idle all the time isn't a situation. Also, he takes three good decisions per day while Warren Buffet advice to take three good decisions a year. Everyone has an art of doing work.

Once a week, Dwayne Johnson - the rock, eats fast food like burgers, pizzas, and anything with family because he carryout a hard workout on rest of the six days. We can enjoy our rest of the time when we become productive in our actual time. That is the real freedom of enjoying real-time. If they have a lot of money, they don't eat anything they want but what they eat what helps them to keep life in shape to enjoy money consistently.

If I'm happy at work, I'm better at home - a better husband & a better father. – Barack Obama

When you stop being productive, you stop being enjoying your money.

Chapter 5

How to Setup Coordination between Conscious and Subconscious Mind

If you always keep looking at the top, you can't set-up the base and blocks.

Humans complain and they complain until they get satisfied with their assumptions. They easily accept situations than to analyze them in a better way. 'You don't know my situations' 'I don't feel like concentrated' 'People bring me down'. **Whenever I interact with people, they have excuses because they have directed their subconscious mind to such problems. When you control your subconscious mind, you control your conscious mind.** People get easily inspired but don't utilize the right power. They get back to their comfort zones as the motivation ends. Even the world's richest people fail sometimes because they try to do something exceptional.

Recently I read a book, **Life without Limits**. It's an autobiography by **Nick Vujicic**, an inspiring man who was born with no arms and no legs. I wept while reading but got inspired at the same time. People don't win by physique but with their mind. He has a rare disorder and apart from it, he's a painter, swimmer, skydiver & motivational speaker. Our subconscious mind is the source of environmental information and it accumulates like hell but it works in coordination. When the subconscious mind supplies the information, the conscious mind accepts it. If it doesn't accept, the subconscious mind throws it somewhere in the corner of our mind. What we feed the most, it supplies us the most. It means our conscious mind bring our subconscious mind into reality. In simple terms, it's like the advertisements by Google. Whatever we see and accept the most while browsing, Google shows us more & direct our mind to it more. When we direct our subconscious mind to positive thoughts, it will start to supply us even more & get increased even more than before.

J.K. Rowling initially started to write in a Nicolson's cafe in which her brother-in-law was owner. She used to see the crowd outside while writing and get fascinated by it. Likewise, some people also get irritated to see the crowd. People throw out what they have the most and what they feed every day. Some people get distressed by the surroundings but sometimes they have to live in it. **The best way of being productive in such an environment is to treat disturbing factors absent.** When you stop being irritated, you will automatically get focused on your work.

Our mind hops from the subconscious to conscious and conscious to subconscious. They are bosom buddy in which consciousness is the pen and subconscious is the blank paper. They work simultaneously.

Chapter 6

The Next Day

The man, who has brilliant tasks the next day, can do the present tasks in a better way.

Being advanced in tasks and planning ahead are much different. A man can be highly productive but till when. It's the problem of human to get inspired easily but habit to not take actions consistently. According to us, God put humans in this world with all the hurdles to know how they will behave in certain situations and we believe, different people behave in different ways. It's not the environment in which they live but their attitude toward it. People say; don't think much about the future but they say it in the context of being happy and stress-free. **Plan your tasks ahead of time to get your mind surrounded by them.** Every time you try to do something drastic, your tasks will make you remind of the goals. Goals are like an alarm clock in our minds. If you feel like you forget the tasks, write them down or paste them somewhere. **Do anything that the productive tasks surround you everywhere.**

Write down your ideas and plans even Bill Gates, the world's richest personality keep track of his notes & ideas. Even the big companies have a track of their records. **When you are trying**

to achieve something substantial, split it into parts; make a diary and carry through it with the help of bijou tasks.

We are really admired by the **quotation of J.K. Rowling**, the wonderful thing about writing is that there is always a blank page waiting. The terrifying thing about writing is that there is always a blank page waiting.

Take gratification from your work and get back to work for consistent pleasure. There's only one element that can give you consistent happiness and peace, the consistent high productive work in the right direction.

Chapter 7

Started High but Forget to Return

One of my friends said, when he's around me, he feels inspired to do something best out of anything. I'm admired by him but that's not the solution to get inspired in everyday life. **We don't need friends to get inspired but need a vision and mindset to return to our work.** People start with strong inspiration to achieve big tasks but such inspiration is of no use. If your inspiration isn't directly proportional to real productivity, don't get inspired. Most tasks remain incomplete because people forget to return to them. Like, there are many writers whose books remain unexecuted for a long time due to various factors. **Keep your work priority high. Take breaks in between the work but return to it as you planned.** Daily tasks get concluded when we take breaks, get energized, and return to it at the right time. Also, some people try to accomplish the whole day task in a few hours. Don't do it. Enjoy while being working with your tasks. Take real breaks, enjoy the time, and return to your work strictly. We are damn sure; you will never get disappointed with your achievements. Really, we are serious about this time.

Instead of doing the hard work, do the right work and split it into few parts of the day. Start great and don't forget to return.

Chapter 8

The Art of Work

Most people say; 'we want to become like him or her. We want to become like our heroes'. **Do you want to become the next Steve Jobs or Elon Musk?** If Warren Buffet reads 500 pages a day, then I will read 600 pages a day. Such statements are vague. We are inspired by people who reflect results in their life. The same work can be done in infinite ways. Everyone has an art of doing work in his way. When people say, you aren't like me; yes exactly we aren't like you. We are like what we really are. Work is not an art; the way people do their work is real art. The different restaurant serves different food in different ways. The same food can be sold for 1 dollar or 1000 dollars. It's the art to allure people to it. **People are already fascinated by Elon Musk, they don't need another but they need people who do work in their ways.** Meanwhile, writing is not an art; the way I bring out emotions through my writing is an art.

Don't try to copy someone just because you like him. There's no point to show audience the same picture again and again. People have break even point to admire the unique art. If they see it frequently, they would lose the charm of attraction.

Don't stand in the queue of others but make your unique style to accomplish the work.

Never try to become like someone but try to get inspired from them and be like yourself. It's better to keep your heroes identity original.

Chapter 9

How to Protect your Time in Unique Ways

We don't have time or we don't schedule our time. There's a big difference.

Suppose, you have 100 best friends, can you talk to all of them every day? Of course not. We can't serve everyone we meet. People don't have time because they don't protect their time. If you want to build knowledge over time, you need a schedule that doesn't suck because of the external environment. We don't say no to our friends because what if they leave us for it. It's significant to make time for our friends but not at the cost of productivity. **These statements look dark but, please accept it as soon as possible.**

Think how Warren Buffet reads 500 pages a day even he has a lot of meetings, friends, tasks, and family. Even when you are a popular personality, people want more of your time. **It's not rude to say no to others but rude to say no to yourself.** One person can set your schedule like he makes own. Now think a hundred persons can make a big mess with your schedule. Remember, they will not protect your time, you have to protect it. Maintain distance with people while being their friends because everyone is in their boat. No one can save us except our time.

Protect your time and don't disturb your revamp with useless things. Warren Buffet is well known for fiercely protecting his time & avoids scheduling meetings or appointments in advance.

Even **Elon Musk** said, '**Keep control of your time. You won't keep control of your time unless you can say no. You can't let other people set your agenda in life.**'

Chapter 10

S trict People

Most people don't become introverts because they feel isolated but when they are surrounded by people, they feel like running a few times. Why! Why!

In between meeting people and doing our work, a situation arises in the life of everyone, what people do when they sit alone. Most people don't know what they do when they are alone because to utilize our empty time, we need a mind that can think in the right direction. Depression, over thinking, anxiety, and no productivity are the results of the horrible use of our alone time. We think; Thinking more isn't a wrong term but over thinking in the wrong direction is the wrong term. Read ahead carefully.

If you count the time, I'm in the office; it's probably no more than 50-60 hours a week. But if you count all the time, I'm focused on our mission, that's basically my whole life. - Mark Zuckerberg.

Everyone thinks all the time. There's no wonder about it but the people who have a purpose can think in the right direction only. We call them strict people with disciplined minds. These people are attached to some goals and link their minds to it every day. Most of the successful people sit alone with relevant goals. They are great introverts to enhance their knowledge every second. Elon Musk was always an introvert & bookish person. Maintain sitting habit with yourself and learn how you behave and think about it. Control, read more books, engage yourself in the right activities, and understand your time.

What is the real truth? - Most successful people have actually no time to waste. They are so much lost in their work that every time they sit alone, they are directed to the purpose and that's the right way to sit, read, & learn.

Chapter 11

A Sense of Urgency

When we are bound by people, we accomplish our work under pressure but when we have the freedom to work in our ways, either we can become lazy or develop a sense of urgency.

The world is developing at a very high pace that every time we read the news, we get something interesting to read. **The most innovative people have no pressure on their work but have a sense of urgency to do their work correctly and in swift ways.** We are experiencing great resources because some people still work round the clock to do it quick and in the possible time.

If today were the last day of your life, would you want to do what you are about to do today? - Steve Jobs.

There's a difference between stupid acts and a sense of urgency. Don't mix both. We aren't telling you to do the tasks as soon as possible but to do tasks quickly to avoid the time wastage in between. A book can be written in one month or one year depends on the urgency of the work. When we develop urgency, we develop the attitude to make our mind to work in that direction. No distractions should be served while achieving a goal and that's how goals are achieved in less time.

Humans have the habit to develop great plans but forget to implement them greatly with a sense of urgency. No one is telling people to do innovation but it's their straightforward utilization of time that makes it great.

Success isn't always about greatness. It's about consistency. Consistent hard work leads to success - **The Rock's Best Advice for Success.**

Chapter 12

The Moment of Being Creative

When you do highly productive work, you already know about it. You don't need opinion from anyone else.

Now a day, people are doing charity on camera and baffling people in private. **People want to conceal the wrong and show the right instead of being neutral in all stages of life.** People don't buy to know who made it but to know how it was made. Some people are highly productive and get desired results but don't enjoy the working process. Of course, it happens in the 21st century. People are getting money for doing their work only. And it happens when they exchange their time with money only. People don't have the moment to enjoy being creative in their work. People are overtired even with everything. **Everything seems spiritless because to live life, they need to be visionary with money.** Like there's art of earning money, there's art of spending money. Everyone should understand the art of spending money on the things that bring the moment of happiness.

Great creations don't need furtherance but only slight visibility. People appreciate & buy the paintings to know how they were made by painters. **A painter enjoys the moment of being creative even in any situation. A writer is lost in his work whether he writes poetry, inspiration, or a sad story.** If someone has to observe the great man who is lost in his work, then we should observe painters and people who observe other people. **Enjoy the moment of being creative in your mood. This is the great way to bring joy in any situations of life.**

Chapter 13

The Elimination of Less Significant

We have heard many times, women take more time to get ready than men and we all accept it very diligently. No issue and no offense. **Everything is significant but if we try to achieve and do everything, we wouldn't get perfection in our real productivity.** We think a quick less time in less significant work can be helpful to give precious time to significant work. People choose what they think important. There's nothing wrong but we should always have the priorities of being best and to utilize productive time in life. Successful people don't waste time to take decisions about what to wear the whole day. They don't give more time to less important work. We aren't telling just because Mark Zuckerberg is following it but it's an indication of how someone can design his goals on a priority basis.

The less important work we do in more time, the less time we would have for productivity and endless low energy for it. A man has to take a lot of decisions in life but not all are important. People have common time usage patterns because they waste their time like everyone else. There are so many salient decisions we have to take & that's why we have to save our energy for it.

There's no shame to eliminate the less important work because there's no logic to give more attention to the less attractive things. That's the smart decision you can ever take. Don't forget. Note it down carefully.

Chapter 14

How to Waste your Time!

If pain is passing in your life, don't stick to it. Let it go as rapid as it can. If pleasure is passing in your life, grab the moment and hold it.

What a foolish chapter! I know you are thinking same in your mind. I haven't lost my consciousness. People are talking about how we should utilize our time and I'm talking about how we should waste our time. Anything you do, we call it art. Everyone does differently. Just like there's an art of spending money, there's also an art of wasting time. People have the habit to hold the moment of pain and endure it entirely. **Don't hold the moments that waste your time. If you want to waste your time, waste it quickly.** Suppose you are wasting five hours of your day in activities you don't even love but regret it later. Don't try to eliminate it in one day. Reduce the time of wastage every day. If you are wasting time while watching TV, then reduce the watch time quickly to have some time for productivity. People waste their time scrolling social media for hours, wandering with people unnecessarily & linger over useless thoughts. **Reduce the time of wastage than to eliminate it forever. There's the reason for this rule.**

If we say someone to leave smoking, he would start to smoke even more than before but if he smokes five cigarettes a day, then he can do sacrifice one cigarette every day for a month, and maybe he will control his habit after that. We can't control by restricting the habit but by giving less freedom to eliminate it forever. Most people try to become productive when they have time but don't forget where we are wasting our time. We should analyze our time well & that's our responsibility.

If you want to waste your time, waste it quickly, and get back to work.

Chapter 15

The Multitaskers

A man can buy five things on his way easily but can't buy two things easily in opposite directions. It takes effort. Don't leave the lesson here, we haven't done talking.

We have a lot of skepticism about how many tasks a single person can do in a single time. And trust me; people have different opinions on it. Some people are multitalented to do studying while watching TV but there's certain combinations work for a series of work. **People drive cars with a lot of functions because all functions are correlated. We believe Multitaskers aren't productive because their productivity divides among the various tasks.** Just at the starting of the chapter, we said, a man can do series of work but each task should be related to each other. All the same type of tasks comes together can build focal point for long time but different tasks can make a big mess & reduce productivity.

Do series of correlated tasks or one task at a time to build focus for a long time. **Don't jump on different tasks but setup coordination between the contrasting tasks.** Also, Multitaskers can be productive but not highly productive if they don't utilize their full potential at one task.

39

'I failed not because I tried something new but because I tried the task that didn't belong to me.'

Chapter 16

Night owls - Not a matter of Debate but a Matter of Solution

It's not about waking up at 5 AM but critical is, what you do at 5 AM. It's not about how early you go to bed but how peacefully you sleep with your time.

We read & learn about many billionaires routines in our life. Some personalities wake up early while some wake up late. Also, some personalities go early to bed while some are night owls. **Everyone is comfortable with the time they think in which they are productive.** Everyone tells us to wake early but no one tells us what we should do in that time except some good personalities like Robin Sharma, Jay Shetty, or Rock. People want to work in high productivity mode when no one else is up and the world is quiet and sleeping. People think anything they do when people are sleeping, can boost their productivity of any kind of work & they think the productivity as pure profit of the day.

Whatever time we choose whether we wake early or going to bed late, we should have strong reasons to sacrifice our time. Sometimes I'm also awakened but I have strong reasons for it. In that time, I do my work honestly and get back to sleep.

We are saying; do not sacrifice your time until you are getting something more of it. The utility of work should be greater than the time you are utilizing. **We can be a night owl or an early bird but until we utilize it strictly with the high utility of work, we can't work like productive personalities.**

If you wake up early, do something that brings peace to your mind. If you are sleeping late, do something relaxing before going to bed.

Chapter 17

Terms to Understand

You can say a lot of things about me, but you cannot say I don't work hard. I don't sing. I don't dance. I don't act. But I'm not lazy. - **Kim Kardashian West.**

When we judge others, we absorb their right and wrong information. When we judge ourselves, we understand our right & wrong & try to make our wrong right.

A **few terms to understand** which is essential for everyone even when they are successful:

1. Money should be secondary when it becomes primary. People invest their time to earn money and stay healthy. Don't lose much time of your time to get money only. Money is the secondary part when we feel like it is our primary part. We enjoy money when we are productive, and go to bed with satisfaction.

2. Your today is not just today; it's the cumulative efforts of your all past days. Our past days aren't useless when we start to learn from them. If we are living today, we should thank and appreciate ourselves to live all the past days.

3. Make it relevant before making it easy. Sometimes people give 100% to the work that requires 10% of the attention. There's no need to make things easy until they are useful to our life. Make it important, and then try to make it easy with your plans.

4. When you can't invest money, invest your mind & every deal will become profitable. The big projects of life don't require money but a real practical mind. The more we use our minds in the right way, the less money we would require. If I can't have money, I will sharpen my mind to reduce the necessity of money.

5. Accomplish every task before going to bed. Many people die with dreams because they don't take early actions. As we said, we need a sense of urgency to treat our everyday sleep like death. Achieve every task before going to bed so we wouldn't get regret leaving our dreams on bullshit procrastination.

6. Don't destroy your schedule for anyone. Keep things and tasks planned & strict. Achieving tasks required a great level of strictness. Be strict with your time, or lose time like every second person. Once we stop being productive, we will start to scrounge the useless things.

7. Don't link productivity with results only. We should link our goals with attributes that don't need people's attention. Link your life with the satisfaction of everyday work and you will never get dissatisfied but will try to make your life better.

8. Original has always more value than beautiful things. People appreciate the real sense of art in the copied world. They have a breakeven point of accepting the copied art. The best way to become unique is to do things as you do. You don't need to change but to accept your way of doing things.

9. No one will celebrate for you. People can join the crowd but we can become productive and satisfied when we do what actually gives us satisfaction. Celebrate your accomplishments before someone congratulate you. The vital disappointment of people is expecting happiness for the work they did for own satisfaction.

10. Many people just do the work but they aren't much curious to do it. A long time healthy environment requires curiosity in the work. Getting bored with our goals is the preliminary stage of getting failed even when no one knows about it.

11. If it doesn't surprise us, it will not surprise anyone. High productivity people don't chase other people's attention but understand how better work they are doing. If it takes away your soul, maybe it will take away people's souls.

12. People think there are secrets to become successful in life. That's not the way. Do the right things, have faith, be consistent, and self-disciplined. Don't be lazy about your tasks.

13. No doesn't mean never. Have the courage to fail. You don't need courage to win, you need courage to fail. - Nick Vujicic.

14. To become highly productive, we have to put something relevant in our minds. Mind's first meal is the first information. Take care of your mind while dealing with others. A sane advice.

Chapter 18

How to Maintain Consistency of Highly Productive Mode

When we climb a mountain, there's less chance of going up. If we lose the grit, we will go down but what we hurt the most in between! Would we climb the mountain again?

If people are fascinated by negativity then they also have the same attraction for positivity. **People think hard work in the right direction brings good results but that's not the real sign. People who are consistent with high productivity have already accepted the assumption of a chance of failure while doing something different.** You know, once Elon Musk lost all his billions while making advanced rockets & spacecrafts for SpaceX. A normal person can't afford to lose 100 bucks on the road. Accept the possibility of every result while doing any work. It's kind of great training to the mind to get to know all the conclusions of a work. Of course, our mind will get hurt when something goes wrong but the recovery will be easy to restore the mode of high productivity. The best successful highly productive personalities have the proficiency to handle any loss with their mind.

The successful people in the stock market aren't the consistent winners but the combination of winning and losing both. We lose our high productive mode when we don't get the desired results. Accept the possibility of everything and do your best, your mind will not get hurt but become a sense to understand the reality of success.

The most loss happens to those who never think about loss. The best success comes to those who accept every result of their work.

Epilogue

I don't know why I'm writing the epilogue. I can't waste my time on useless even while I have said everything with my high productivity mode. **Don't waste your time and if you are still wasting, waste it quickly, and I think, that's the smallest epilogue you have ever read in any book.**

About the Author

THE **Bestselling** Author **Deepak Gupta** is best known for writing plain sailing, meticulous, and pragmatic Self-Help books. He's the author of **more than forty books** including **10 Principles to Beat Failure** that won **Google Best Choice 2018** & became **Top Seller on Google Play Store in 2019.** He has garnered much acclaim for his **30 Minutes Read & 10 Principles Series.** Till now, he has received **500k+ readership** & **a lot of appreciation** from all over the world.

Deepak Gupta received his post-graduation degree from **Delhi School of Economics.** Also, when he's not writing, he can be found wandering on his **exquisite terrace garden.** He lives with his family in **Delhi, India.** You can get to know about him by typing the words **'Author Deepak Gupta'** into Google. No, seriously, try it.

Keep in touch with Deepak via the web:

Instagram: https://www.instagram.com/authordeepakgupta/

Website: https://www.authordeepakgupta.com/

Facebook: https://www.facebook.com/authordeepakgupta

Twitter: https://twitter.com/authordeepakgup

New Book Alert: https://books2read.com/author/deepak-gupta/subscribe/1/86268/

Don't miss out!

Visit the website below and you can sign up to receive emails whenever Deepak Gupta publishes a new book. There's no charge and no obligation.

https://books2read.com/r/B-A-AQXE-QHRLB

BOOKS 2 READ

Connecting independent readers to independent writers.

Did you love *The Rules of Being Highly Productive*? Then you should read *10 Principles To Beat Failure: Illustrated Enhanced Edition 2021*[1] by Deepak Gupta!

[2]

Implement drop in the ocean of knowledge and you can make ocean out of the drop.

Life is not as plain-sailing as we think. It has the habit to create hurdles in our path. Whenever we try to do something great, people will come and laugh at us. This is the universal law. 10 Principles to Beat Failure can help you with the following Concepts & Problems:

How to be Happy Consistently.Problems related Truths &

---

1. https://books2read.com/u/m0gvyY

2. https://books2read.com/u/m0gvyY

Myths.How to execute plans.How to feel satisfied at the end of day.How to set your Goals Strongly.How to say NO to unwanted tasks.How to understand Rights & Wrongs to Success.Why we fail at execution of Goals.Do's & Don'ts in Morning Schedule.How to understand your Satisfaction Level.How to be Successful Consistently.How to build Bullet-Proof Success.How to Celebrate Success.How to Increase Knowledge.The Attributes of Visionary People.How to Free your Mind.The Classical Conditioning of Life.How to Work in Panic.How to Link Appreciation with Results.How to attract more people to our products.How to not be a Rat.The Bandersnatch to take Best Life Decisions.How to get more ideas everyday.The Game of Mindset.How to decide our Mind Feed.

What to expect in NEW ILLUSTRATED ENHANCED EDITION 2021:

★ Added 32 New Chapters, Bonuses, and Illustrations which will help readers to understand Success and Failure Principles in much Simplified Manner.

★ Revised All Principles with Best Possible Practical Practices.

Every day is the day to get up again and to learn something innovative and creative. To become a superior person, we should learn to observe our nature and understand the latent power inside it. Our power lies in to understand the invincible love and greatest power of our mind. But how much we focus to create our mind happy and healthy? Have we ever thought of this matter? How many negative thoughts have unconsciously latent in our mind? How we waste our energy every day because of our purposeless negative thoughts. We never focus on the depth of our mind as we always busy in our run and races &

money and faces. Being good is not only a matter of the good heart but also the matter of the beautiful mind to cope up with the end number of life failures. If you want to become cheery and to take the right decision, then you should understand the beautiful nerves of your mind.

10 Principles To Beat Failure includes ten mind boggling principles that will change your life forever and boost you to achieve your dreams and aspirations at any stage of life.

We have to ask questions, not because we want to know the answers. Answers don't exist universally. They exist in the form to make fit in our life. What make us satisfied is our answers.

Read more at https://www.authordeepakgupta.com.

Also by Deepak Gupta

30 Minutes Read
One Second Rule: How to take Right Decisions quickly
without Thinking too Much
Hard Decisions Easy Life: Bandersnatch & the World of
Possibilities
Sell Your Talent: How to Convert Talent into Money along
with the Personality Development
Ideas & Origami
The Anti-Suicidal Self Help Book
The Therapy of Peace: Illustrated Edition
The Habit of Positivity

Power
The Power of Universe: Your Sun will Rise when your Sky
appears Blue
The Power of Nothing: They say and We do

Standalone

Inspiring Life

She: She heals everything

She: She Heals Everything

The Universe Of Your Mind

10 Principles To Beat Failure: Illustrated Enhanced Edition 2021

She's the Sunflower: Heart Healing Poetry and Prose

10 Principles To Love Yourself: How to Start your Day and Sleep Peacefully

How To Heal Yourself

She: She heals everything

Skyfall: Your Heart Will Fall Too

The Girl With No Dreams

The Pigeon With Broken Legs: Modern Classics Children Story

Average Mind: The World is not the Wonder. It's the Wonder which makes your World

Being Busy Is Not Always Productive: Stop Wasting your Time at the Wrong Place

Powerful Quotes: Quotes That Make You Think

Happiness Without Cause: Why Happiness was easy in the 19th Century but not in the 21st Century

Alone Than Lonely: How to Live Life without Attachment & Enjoy your Company

The Lost Child

When Queen Drowns

The Power Pack of Short Stories: Box Set of Crime, Thriller & Suspense Stories

Average Mind | The Power of Nothing | 10 Principles To Beat Failure | 10 Principles To Love Yourself |: Box Set

How To Deal With Haters: Understand the Thin Line of Thinking Process with 99% Theory

Amazon Kindle & Google Play ebooks Pricing System: Maximize Your ebooks Sales

5 Principles To Dig Out Success: The Rules of Start, Roller coaster, Visibility, Stickiness, & Interstices

Two Friends in a Boat

????: Udhaar

The Little Book of Wise Quotes

The Rules of Being Highly Productive

Watch for more at https://www.authordeepakgupta.com.